Halloween

by Pearl Markovics

Consultant:
Beth Gambro
Reading Specialist
Yorkville, Illinois

Contents

BEARPORT
PUBLISHING

New York, New York

Halloween

What day is it?

It is Halloween!

It is Halloween.

I see the cats.

It is Halloween.

I see the ghosts.

It is Halloween.

I see the treats.

It is Halloween.

I see the spiders.

It is Halloween.

I see the pumpkins.

It is Halloween.

What do you see?

Key Words

cats

ghosts

pumpkins

spiders

treats

Index

About the Author

Pearl Markovics loves holidays of
every kind—especially the ones that include
sweets and lots of presents.

Teaching Tips

Before Reading

✔ Guide readers on a "picture walk" through the text by asking them to name the things shown.

✔ Discuss book structure by showing children where text will appear consistently on pages.

✔ Highlight the supportive pattern of the book. Note the consistent number of sentences and words found on each page.

During Reading

✔ Encourage children to "read with your finger" and point to each word as it is read. Stop periodically to ask readers to point to a specific word in the text.

✔ Reading strategies: When encountering unknown words, prompt readers with encouraging cues, such as:

- **Does that word look like a word you already know?**
- **It could be _____ , but look at _____ .**
- **Check the picture.**

After Reading

✔ Write the key words on index cards.

- **Have readers match them to pictures in the book.**
- **Have children sort words by category (words that are six letters long, for example).**

✔ Encourage readers to talk about other holidays.

✔ Ask readers to identify their favorite page in the book. Have them read that page aloud.

✔ Ask children to write their own sentences about a holiday. Encourage them to use the same pattern found in the book as a model for their writing.

Credits: Cover, © David Carillet/Shutterstock, © sandsun/Shutterstock, and © karamysh/Shutterstock; 1, © unverdorben jr/Shutterstock; 2–3, © mediaphotos/iStock; 4–5, © Chirtsova Natalia/Shutterstock and © Eric Isselee/Shutterstock; 6–7, © Kzenon/Shutterstock; 8–9, © Arinahabich/iStock; 10–11, © CBW/Alamy; 12–13, © David Carillet/Shutterstock; 14–15, © Luis Louro/Shutterstock; 16T (L to R), © Chirtsova Natalia/Shutterstock, © Eric Isselee/Shutterstock, and © Kzenon/Shutterstock; 16B (L to R), © David Carillet/Shutterstock, © CBW/Alamy, and © Arinahabich/iStock.

Publisher: Kenn Goin   **Senior Editor**: Joyce Tavolacci   **Creative Director**: Spencer Brinker

Library of Congress Cataloging-in-Publication Data in process at time of publication (2019)
Library of Congress Control Number: 2018023583
ISBN-13: 978-1-64280-116-3 (library binding) | ISBN-13: 978-1-64280-151-4 (paperback)

10 9 8 7 6 5 4 3 2 1